I Can Read GOD'S WORD!

The Lord is My Shepherd

and other stories from the Psalms

BARBOUR
PUBLISHING

PHIL A. SMOUSE

In him was life,
and that life was the light of men.

John 1:4 NIV

ISBN 1-59310-102-3

Published by Barbour Publishing, Inc., P.O. Box 719, Uhrichsville, Ohio 44683
www.barbourbooks.com

Our mission is to publish and distribute inspirational products offering exceptional value and biblical encouragement to the masses.

Member of the
Evangelical Christian
Publishers Association

Printed in China.
5 4 3 2

CONTENTS

A NOTE TO PARENTS. . .

I Can Read God's Word! is a simple idea with a simple goal: to put the Word of God on the lips of God's children.

I've drawn from the practical teachings of Jesus in the New Testament and the promises of God in the Old and "translated" them into an easy-to-read paraphrase that is absolutely faithful to the original text while staying as close as possible to the phonics-based reading curriculum your children are learning at home or in school.

Twenty-three long years went by before I ever read a single page of the Bible for myself. But if God answers prayer (and you know He does), before *this* year is over you will hear a familiar little voice say, "Mom, Dad, listen. . .*I Can Read God's Word!*"

Enjoy!

Phil A. Smouse

MY SHEPHERD

Psalm 23

The Lord is
my shepherd.

I will always have
everything I need.

We will lie down
in green grass.

We will walk
by quiet water.

God will give me
peace in my soul.

Because God loves me
He will lead me.

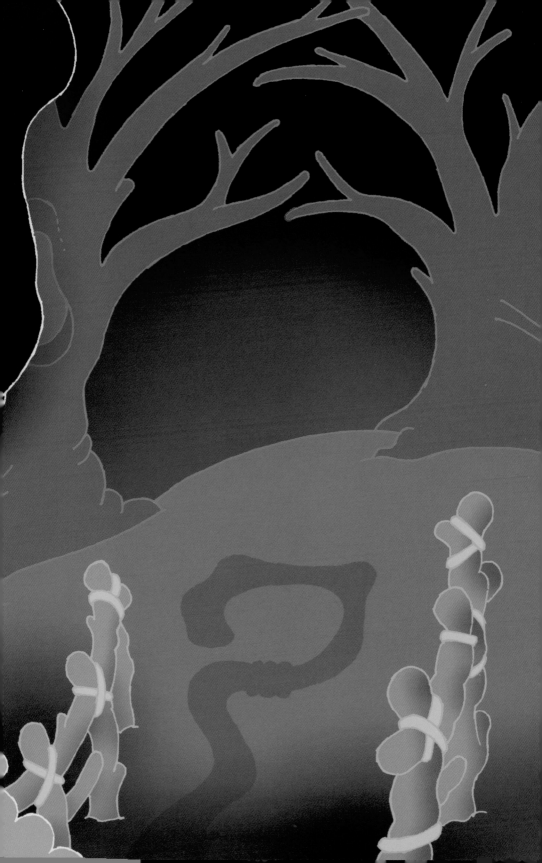

Even when I am in
a dark and scary place
I will not be afraid.
God is with me.

His rod will show me
where to walk.

His staff will keep me safe.

His love will wipe
away my tears.

Enemies may be all around me.

But I will eat
in peace and safety.
I am the Lord's
welcome guest.

My cup will run over!

God's goodness
and love will be with me
every day of my life.

And I will live
in God's house
forever.

THE HEAVENS DECLARE!

Psalm 19:1-4

The heavens shout,
"God is great!"

The sky cries out,

"I was made by God's hand!"

Day after day it
speaks of God's goodness.

Night after night
it sings praise to God.

And God says,
"*I love you*"
all over the world!

YOUR HEART'S DESIRE

Psalm 37:3-4

Trust the Lord
and do good!

Live and be happy.
You are God's child.

Make the Lord
your greatest joy,

and He will give you
your heart's desire.

UNDER HIS WINGS

Psalm 91:1, 4, 14-16

God loves me.
And I love Him!
His love has
set me free.

When I call Him
He will answer.

When I am afraid

He will comfort me.

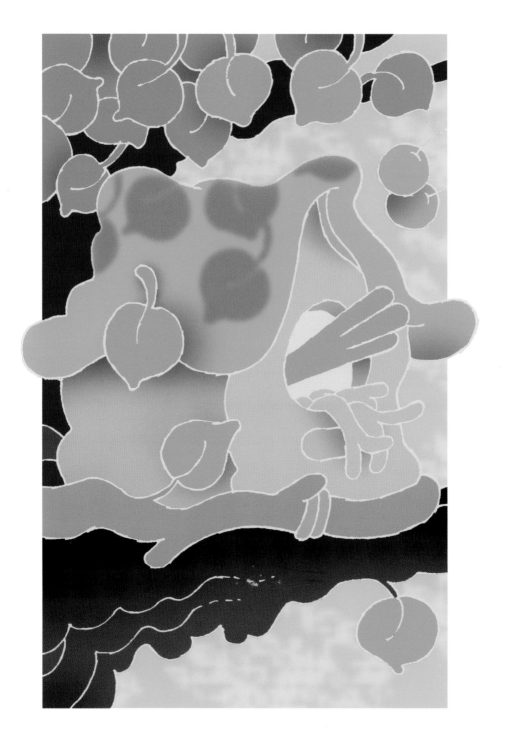

I will make my
home with God.
I will be safe
in God's shadow.

For I am in a good
and happy place
under God's wings.

MY SHEPHERD

Psalm 23

The LORD is my shepherd; I shall not want. He makes me to lie down in green pastures; He leads me beside the still waters. He restores my soul; He leads me in the paths of righteousness for His name's sake. Yea, though I walk through the valley of the shadow of death, I will fear no evil; for You are with me; Your rod and Your staff they comfort me. You prepare a table before me in the presence of my enemies; you anoint my head with oil; my cup runs over. Surely goodness and mercy shall follow me all the days of my life; and I will dwell in the house of the LORD forever.

THE HEAVENS DECLARE

Psalm 19:1–4

The heavens declare the glory of God; and the firmament shows His handiwork. Day unto day utters speech, and night unto night reveals knowledge. There is no speech nor language where their voice is not heard. Their line has gone out through all the earth, and their words to the end of the world.

YOUR HEART'S DESIRE

Psalm 37:3–4

Trust in the LORD, and do good; dwell in the land, and feed on His faithfulness. Delight yourself also in the LORD, and He shall give you the desires of your heart.

UNDER HIS WINGS

Psalm 91:1, 4, 14–16

He who dwells in the secret place of the Most High shall abide under the shadow of the Almighty. He shall cover you with His feathers, and under His wings you shall take refuge. Because he has set his love upon Me, therefore I will deliver him. . . . He shall call upon Me, and I will answer him; I will be with him in trouble; I will deliver him and honor him. With long life I will satisfy him, and show him My salvation.